HAMMOND

my first atlas

Mapmakers for the 21st Century

CONTENTS

THE WORLD

THE WORLD is round. So, to make a map of the world appear on a flat page, the world's curved surface must be flattened out and parts of it stretched. The world map *(below)* is the result. The maps in this atlas show different areas of the world. Look for the little world map printed on each page. The part shaded red shows where in the world that area is situated.

Greenla...

NORTH
AMERICA

Rocky Mts.

ATLANTI·

OCEAN

Hawaiian Is.

PACIFIC OCEAN

Equator

Galápagos
Is.

Amazon

Andes

SOUTH
AMERICA

French
Polynesia

Scale

0   2,500 miles

HOW TO USE THIS ATLAS

The maps in this atlas have been specially drawn to show where different kinds of landscape are found.

	Arctic lands (tundra)		Forest and woodlands		Grassland
	Mountains		Coniferous forest		Marshes
	Desert		Farmland		Rivers and lakes

A scale bar *(below)* tells us how far distances on the map are in the real world. You can use it to work out longer or shorter distances.

Scale

0   100 miles

Boundaries between countries are shown in this atlas by red lines *(below left)*. Boundaries between states within countries, or disputed boundaries, are both shown by broken lines *(below right)*.

ARCTIC OCEAN

Svalbard

Iceland

EUROPE

Ural Mts.

Ob

ASIA

Gobi

Himalayas

Sahara Desert

Nile

AFRICA

Seychelles

INDIAN

OCEAN

Aleutian Is.

PACIFIC OCEAN

Hawaiian Is.

Marshall Is.

Kiribati

New Guinea

Solomon Is.

Samoa

Fiji

Tonga

New Caledonia

AUSTRALIA

New Zealand

Kergeulen Is.

Killer whales swim in the Arctic seas.

This pipeline carries oil across Alaska. It is built above the ground so that caribou can pass underneath it.

ALASKA
(US)

Yukon

ARCTIC
OCEAN

Banks
Island

Victoria
Island

ANCHORAGE

YUKON
TERRITORY

Mackenzie

Great Bear
Lake

PACIFIC OCEAN

NORTHWEST
TERRITORIES

NUNAVUT

Rocky

Great Slave
Lake

DID YOU KNOW . . ?

Canada has two languages, English and French. The French were the first Europeans to settle Canada but the British won control after a war. French is still spoken in the province of Québec, English elsewhere.

C   A   N   A   D   A

BRITISH
COLUMBIA

Mountains

ALBERTA

EDMONTON

MANITOBA

SASKATCHEWAN

VANCOUVER

CALGARY

Saskatchewan

REGINA

WINNIPEG

For many years, the native peoples of Canada's western coast carved totem poles. The poles stand at the doorways of their village homes. The wood carvings show figures and animals that were important in the history of their families.

CANADA AND THE ARCTIC

CANADA is the second largest country in the world, after Russia. The northern region of Canada, known as tundra, is a frozen wasteland for about nine months of the year. Further south lie vast coniferous forests. Rising in the west are the craggy Rocky and Coast Mountains. Nearly all of Canada's cities lie close to the border with the USA and in the fertile grasslands known as the prairies. Alaska, a state of the USA, is a land of tundra and forests.

GREENLAND
(Denmark)

BAFFIN BAY

Baffin Island

HUDSON BAY

ATLANTIC OCEAN

NEWFOUNDLAND

QUÉBEC

St. Lawrence

ONTARIO

NEW BRUNSWICK

PR. EDWARD I.

NOVA SCOTIA

Lake Superior

QUÉBEC

MONTRÉAL

Lake Huron

OTTAWA

TORONTO

L. Ontario

L. Erie

Scale

0   400 miles

The Canadian Pacific Railway was completed more than 100 years ago. It links Canada's eastern and western coasts. Here, it crosses the spectacular Rocky Mountains. The trains mostly carry cargo, although the route is also popular with tourists.

The Inuit live in northern Canada and Greenland. Many Inuit still hunt whales, seals and caribou. Nowadays they use modern equipment such as snowmobiles and rifles.

UNITED STATES OF AMERICA

THE United States of America stretches from Atlantic to Pacific coasts of North America. The eastern USA is made up of the wooded Appalachian Mountains and fertile plains. The center of the country, the Mississippi lowlands, is mainly farmland. In the west, the landscape is mountainous. Here the climate, apart from on the Pacific coast, is much drier.

Once settled only by Native Americans, the USA is now home to people who came from all over the world to live here.

Scale
0   300 miles

SEATTLE
WASHINGTON
MONTANA
OREGON
IDAHO
ROCKY Mts
Snake
WYOMING
SALT LAKE CITY
NEVADA
DENVER
UTAH
COLORA
San Francisco
CALIFORNIA
Colorado
PACIFIC OCEAN
LOS ANGELES
ARIZONA
NEW MEXICO
PHOENIX
Rio G

Baseball is a popular summer sport in the USA. It is played between two teams of nine players on a diamond-shaped field. Batters attempt to strike a ball thrown towards them by a pitcher.

The centers of many American cities are often crowded with skyscrapers. Seattle, in the northwest, also has the Space Needle. From the top there is a superb view of the city and the mountains nearby.

HONOLULU

HAWAII

The Everglades, a large area of wetlands in southern Florida, are a haven for rare animals such as alligators and wading birds. Some people want to drain part of the land for farms.

NORTH DAKOTA

MINNESOTA

Lake Superior

MAINE

MINNEAPOLIS

WISCONSIN

MICHIGAN

Lake Huron

Lake Ontario

VT.

N.H.

BOSTON

CONN.	CONNECTICUT
N.H.	NEW HAMPSHIRE
MASS.	MASSACHUSETTS
MD.	MARYLAND
R.I.	RHODE ISLAND
VT.	VERMONT

SOUTH DAKOTA

L. Michigan

NEW YORK

MASS.

R.I.

CONN.

IOWA

DETROIT

L. Erie

NEW YORK

NEBRASKA

Missouri

CHICAGO

CLEVELAND

PENNSYLVANIA

NEW JERSEY

PHILADELPHIA

INDIANA

OHIO

WASHINGTON

KANSAS CITY

ILLINOIS

Ohio

WEST VIRGINIA

MD.

DELAWARE

The Statue of Liberty stands on an island at the entrance to New York Harbor. The huge copper statue was built as a gift of friendship from France to the USA.

KANSAS

ST. LOUIS

MISSOURI

KENTUCKY

VIRGINIA

Arkansas

ARKANSAS

TENNESSEE

NORTH CAROLINA

Appalachian Mts.

OKLAHOMA

Mississippi

ALABAMA

ATLANTA

SOUTH CAROLINA

ATLANTIC OCEAN

DALLAS

MISSISSIPPI

GEORGIA

TEXAS

LOUISIANA

NEW ORLEANS

FLORIDA

HOUSTON

GULF OF MEXICO

MIAMI

Cotton is an important crop in the south. It was once hand-picked by black slaves brought by force from Africa. Now modern machines do the job.

Much of northern Mexico is covered by desert. The cactus is often the only plant life here.

Mexico City, the capital of Mexico, lies at more than 6,500 feet above sea level. With more than 20 million people, it is one of the largest cities in the world—and one of the most polluted.

MEXICALI

Sierra Madre

GULF OF CALIFORNIA

Río Grande

Scale

0   250 miles

MONTERREY

M E X I C O

GULF OF MEXICO

GUADALAJARA

MÉRIDA

MEXICO CITY

In many Central American and Caribbean countries, growing bananas is the most important industry. As the bananas grow, workers cover them with bags to protect them from insects. The bananas are cut down while they are still green. They ripen just before they go on sale.

BELIZE

GUATEMALA

EL SALVADOR

PACIFIC OCEAN

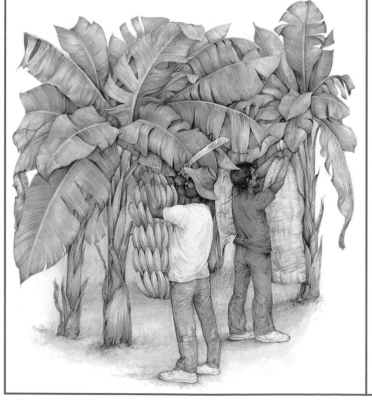

The Panama Canal links the Atlantic and Pacific Oceans. Before the canal was built, ships had to go around in the stormy seas off the southern tip of South America. A series of locks were built to take canal traffic across the 50-mile stretch of land. Small trains help pull the ships through the locks.

Hand weaving is an ancient Indian art that still goes on in Mexico and Guatemala. Each region has its own style.

MEXICO AND CENTRAL AMERICA

MEXICO and the Central American countries stretch from the United States in the north to South America in the south. A mountain chain runs all the way down. There are many active volcanoes and the land is regularly shaken by earthquakes too. In the north the climate is dry, but further south there is tropical rainforest.

The Caribbean islands have a tropical climate. They often suffer fierce hurricanes.

BAHAMAS

HAVANA

TURKS & CAICOS IS. (Br.)

ANGUILLA (Br.)

VIRGIN IS. (Br. & US)

ANTIGUA

CUBA

ST. KITTS & NEVIS

GUADELOUPE (Fr.)

DOMINICAN REPUBLIC

HAITI

PUERTO RICO (US)

DOMINICA

MARTINIQUE (Fr.)

ST. LUCIA

JAMAICA

BARBADOS

ST. VINCENT AND THE GRENADINES

GRENADA

CARIBBEAN SEA

NETHERLANDS ANTILLES

TRINIDAD AND TOBAGO

ONDURAS

CARAGUA

Panama Canal

COSTA RICA

PANAMA

Steel band music is popular on every Caribbean island. It was first played in Trinidad. The pans or drums are made from large oil drums. Calypso and Reggae music both have their origins in the Caribbean.

9

SOUTH AMERICA

T HE CLIMATE in the northern part of South America is hot and rainy. The great Amazon Rainforest fills the Amazon River basin, a vast lowland area lying between the Andes and the Brazilian Highlands. The Andes mountains stretch all the way down the western edge of the continent to its cold, stormy southern tip, Cape Horn. Most of South America's farmland and cities are in the east, in southeastern Brazil and northern Argentina.

DID YOU KNOW ..?

The Amazon River is about 4,000 miles long. It carries more water than any other river—more than the world's eight longest rivers put together.

These Indians take home their catch—an anaconda.

Scale

0   350 miles

RECIFE

BRAZIL

Brazilian Highlands

Amazon Rainforest

Amazon

Madeira

Negro

FRENCH GUIANA

SURINAME

GUYANA

VENEZUELA

Orinoco

CARACAS

COLOMBIA

BOGOTÁ

ECUADOR

QUITO

P E R Ú

LIMA

BOLIVIA

LA PAZ

L. Titicaca

PACIFIC OCEAN

RIO DE JANEIRO

Mardi Gras, or Fat Tuesday, is a time of carnival in Rio de Janeiro, Brazil. There are parties and balls. People dress up in amazing costumes and parade through the streets.

These children live in a shantytown on the edge of one of South America's huge cities. There are not enough places for poorer people to live in the cities, so many build their own houses out of spare pieces of iron and wood.

SÃO PAULO

Paraná

PARAGUAY

URUGUAY

MONTEVIDEO

BUENOS AIRES

ARGENTINA

SANTIAGO

C

H   I   L

E

Andes

ATLANTIC OCEAN

Falkland Is. (Br.)

Tierra del Fuego

Patagonia

Cape Horn

A condor glides without flapping its wings for many miles over the barren and remote southern Andes Mountains.

Indian peoples who live in the mountains of Peru and Bolivia still have their traditional dress and customs.

The Berbers come from Morocco. Each year, Berber girls dress in a special costume and go to a ceremony where they are chosen as brides.

The Wodaabe people of Niger live by herding cattle and sheep in the dry grasslands close to the Sahara Desert. The men wear special make-up for performing a courtship dance.

MEDITERRANEAN SEA

ATLANTIC OCEAN

CASABLANCA

ALGIERS

TUNIS

TUNISIA

MOROCCO

Atlas Mountains

ALGERIA

LI

WESTERN SAHARA

Sahara De

MAURITANIA

MALI

NIGER

DAKAR

SENEGAL

THE GAMBIA

Niger

Lake Chad

GUINEA-BISSAU

BURKINA FASO

GUINEA

SIERRA LEONE

BENIN

NIGERIA

CÔTE D'IVOIRE

GHANA

TOGO

LAGOS

LIBERIA

ACCRA

CAMEROON

GULF OF GUINEA

EQUATORIAL GUINEA

DID YOU KNOW . . ?

Most of the Sahara Desert is not sandy at all, but covered with rock and gravel. At night, it is usually freezing cold.

The ancient Egyptian pyramids are about 4,500 years old.

NORTHERN AFRICA

THE SAHARA is the largest hot desert in the world. It stretches right across North Africa, from the Atlantic Ocean to the Red Sea. The only river that runs across it is the Nile, the world's longest river. The Nile has farmland close to its banks.

If you travel south from the Sahara, you will come across grassy plains. Near the West African coast there is some thick rainforest, although many trees have been cut down to make more room for farmland.

Scale

0   500 miles

Y A
r t

EGYPT

CAIRO

RED SEA

Nile

A D

KHARTOUM

ERITREA

S U D A N

DJIBOUTI

ADDIS ABABA

CENTRAL AFRICAN REPUBLIC

E T H I O P I A

S O M A L I A

The Sahara is a vast, dry desert. But there are some places where water can be found. These are called oases.

This is a fruit market in West Africa. People carrying containers around on their heads are a common sight.

Many Africans follow the traditional religions of their ancestors. Their worship involves dances in which special clothes and masks, like this one from Congo, are worn.

Strange trees called baobabs or "bottle trees" grow on Madagascar. Their trunks store water in the dry months.

CONGO

GABON

DEMOCRATIC REPUBLIC OF THE CONGO

Congo

Kasai

(Angola)

KINSHASA

LUANDA

ATLANTIC OCEAN

ANGOLA

UGANDA

KENYA

Lake Victoria

RWANDA

BURUNDI

NAIROBI

TANZANIA

DAR ES SALAAM

Lake Nyasa

LUBUMBASHI

MALAWI

ZAMBIA

LUSAKA

MOZAMBIQUE

Zambezi

HARARE

ZIMBABWE

Namib Desert

BOTSWANA

Kalahari Desert

Limpopo

NAMIBIA

MOZAMBIQUE

JOHANNESBURG

MAPUTO

SWAZILAND

Orange

SOUTH AFRICA

LESOTHO

Cape of Good Hope

Scale

0   500 miles

CAPE TOWN

The Maasai people come from East Africa, where they herd cattle. They wear the same beautiful ornaments that their ancestors did centuries ago. Girls older than nine adorn themselves with colorful necklaces and fantastic earrings.

SOUTHERN AFRICA

THE SOUTHERN half of Africa also has deserts: the Kalahari and the Namib in the southwest. But most of the region is covered either by rainforest, in the Congo Basin, or dry grasslands. The Great Rift Valley, a long "crack" in the Earth's surface, runs down through East Africa, a region of mountains, volcanoes and long lakes.

Africa is famous for the huge variety of animals that roam across its plains. Giraffes, wildebeests, elephants, zebras and rhinoceroses live here, along with predators such as lions, cheetahs and hyenas.

Many countries of Southern Africa are rich in copper, diamonds, gold and other minerals. Miners drill the rock deep below the surface. Many local people are employed in the mines.

INDIAN

OCEAN

COMOROS

NTANANARIVO

1ADAGASCAR

DID YOU KNOW . . ?

Thousands of tourists visit Africa's wildlife parks, where the animals are protected by law. Unfortunately, many animals, such as elephants and rhinos, are killed by poachers, who then cut off and sell their tusks and horns. Some animals are now endangered.

Savannah, dry grassland with open woodland, covers the East African plains. Herds of animals, such as giraffes and zebras, live here.

WESTERN EUROPE

THE WESTERN lands of Europe stretch from the windy, wet Shetlands in the far north to the hot southern coasts of Spain and Portugal. The Atlantic Ocean brings cooling breezes in summer, but also mild weather in winter. The western coasts of the British Isles, Brittany and northwestern Spain have quite frequent rainfall. In the warmer, drier areas of France, Spain and Portugal, the climate is perfect for vineyards.

Amsterdam, capital of the Netherlands, is a city of fine old houses, canals and bridges.

Shetland Is.

NORTH SEA

SCOTLAND

UNITED KINGDOM

GLASGOW

NORTHERN IRELAND

DUBLIN

IRELAND

MANCHESTER

ENGLAND

BIRMINGHAM

WALES

LONDON

ENGLISH CHANNEL

BRITTANY

NETHERLANDS

AMSTERDAM

BELGIUM

BRUSSELS

LUXEMBOURG

Meuse

PARIS

Seine

Loire

FRANCE

The building of Stonehenge, England, was begun about 3500 BC, 1,000 years before the pyramids in Egypt. It may have been a place to observe the stars, or a temple of worship. The stones were quarried 180 miles away.

The game of *pétanque* is very popular in France. It is played in most towns and villages. The object is to throw your ball as close as possible to a smaller ball.

ALps

MONACO

Corsica

Rhône

MARSEILLE

MEDITERRANEAN
SEA

BAY OF BISCAY

BORDEAUX

Garonne

ANDORRA

P y r e n e e s

Ebro

BARCELONA

Mallorca

VALENCIA

Balearic Islands

BILBAO

Duero

S P A I N

Tagus

MADRID

Guadalquivir

SEVILLE

Gibraltar (Br.)

PORTO

P O R T U G A L

ATLANTIC
OCEAN

LISBON

Scale

0 ———— 150 miles

DID YOU KNOW . . ?

**The United Kingdom,
France, Netherlands,
Spain and Portugal
have all at one time
possessed great
overseas empires. In
fact, nearly all of the
Americas, Africa,
Oceania and much of
southern and south-
eastern Asia have been
ruled by one of these
nations at some time in
their history.**

Forests of evergreen
oak trees cover about
one third of Portugal.
The bark of these
trees is used to make
cork. It is stripped off
and left to dry. Then
it is steamed or
boiled and pressed
into sheets ready for
use. The trees may
provide cork bark for
100 years or more.

The cathedral of La
Sagrada Familia (the
Sacred Family) is one
of the most amazing
sights in Barcelona.
Still unfinished
today, it is a building
of soaring towers and
decorated stonework.

SOUTHERN EUROPE

THE LANDS of southern Europe border the Mediterranean and Black Seas. Italy and Greece are made up of peninsulas and islands. Rivers such as the Danube and its tributaries, and the River Po in northern Italy, flow across wide fertile plains, but most of southern Europe is hilly or mountainous.

The ancient Greek civilization and the Roman Empire both began and spread across this region. Many historic remains still stand today.

The Parliament Building of Hungary stands on the eastern side of the River Danube in the capital, Budapest.

Building work began on the bell tower next to the Cathedral at Pisa, Italy, more than 800 years ago. Unfortunately, the ground beneath it was too soft and the tower began to lean. Today, engineers have made sure the Leaning Tower of Pisa will not fall over.

HU

SLOVENIA ZAGREB

MILAN VENICE

TURIN Po

C R O A T I A

Sava

SAN MARINO

BOSNIA AND HERZEGOV

SARAJEVO

A L P S

A

I T A L Y

A D R I A T I C   S E A

ROME

Sardinia

NAPLES

TYRRHENIAN SEA

Sicily

MALTA M E D I T E R

Marshes grow along the banks of the Danube near its mouth. Here, white pelicans come to nest in large numbers. They use their pouched bills to catch fish.

The ruins of buildings that were once magnificent temples are found all over Greece. This is Delphi, built on the slopes of Mount Parnassus. For the ancient Greeks, it was an important place of worship.

Southeast Europe is home to many different peoples and religions. This is a Muslim girl from Bosnia and Herzegovina.

DID YOU KNOW . . ?

The smallest country in the world is the Vatican City State. About one eighth the size of Central Park, in New York, it lies inside Rome, capital of Italy. The Vatican is the home of the Pope. It has its own newspaper, bank and railway station.

NORTHERN EUROPE

ORWAY, Sweden and Denmark are known as Scandinavia. Together with Finland, they are the most northerly European lands. Central Europe lies between the Baltic Sea and the Alps. The plains of northern Germany, Denmark and Poland are fertile. Evergreen forests cover upland areas, as well as low-lying Finland.

These sea inlets in Norway's coastline are called fjords.

Lapland is home to the Lapps, or Saami people. A few still herd reindeer, a traditional way of life.

Scale

0 150 miles

DID YOU KNOW . . . ?
Northern Scandinavia is the Land of the Midnight Sun. At the height of summer, the sun never sets. But in the depths of winter, it never rises.

FINLAND

OULU

TALLINN

ESTONIA

HELSINKI

Åland

GULF OF BOTHNIA

Inari

LAPLAND

SWEDEN

STOCKHOLM

Vänern

NORWAY

TRONDHEIM

BERGEN

OSLO

ICELAND

REYKJAVIK

Mountains cover much of Austria and Switzerland. Many Austrian village churches have onion-shaped domes.

The River Rhine in Germany is a major waterway. Barges carry goods up and down it. They pass through the Rhine gorge, a land of castles and vine-covered slopes.

This man shapes a blob of melted glass by blowing into it. Glassblowing is a traditional industry of Poland.

LATVIA

RIGA

LITHUANIA

VILNIUS

(RUSSIA)

BALTIC SEA

DENMARK

COPENHAGEN

Bornholm

WARSAW

Vistula

P O L A N D

GDANSK

HAMBURG

BERLIN

Elbe

G E R M A N Y

FRANKFURT

COLOGNE

Rhine

KRAKOW

PRAGUE

CZECH REPUBLIC

S L O V A K I A

BRATISLAVA

VIENNA

A U S T R I A

Danube

MUNICH

LIECHTENSTEIN

A l p s

ZURICH

SWITZERLAND

GENEVA

RUSSIA AND CENTRAL ASIA

RUSSIA is the largest country in the world. It stretches across two continents, Europe and Asia. Most of its people live in the European part, to the west of the Ural Mountains. Siberia, the Asian part, is a land of mountains and forests. It is bitterly cold for much of the year.

This train travels on the Trans–Siberian Railway, the longest railway in the world. A trip from Moscow to Vladivostok takes eight days.

DID YOU KNOW . . ?

Lake Baikal is the deepest lake in the world. From surface to bottom, it is four times the height of the tallest skyscraper.

Novaya Zemlya

L. Ladoga

ST. PETERSBURG

ARKHANGELSK

MINSK

BELARUS

MOSCOW

KIEV

MOLDOVA

UKRAINE

KHARKOV

ROSTOV

Volga

SAMARA

Ural Mountains

YEKATERINBURG

Ob

R U S S I

Trans-Siberian Railway

OMSK

GEORGIA

ARMENIA

(AZER-BAIJAN)

AZER-BAIJAN

Caspian Sea

BAKU

KAZAKHSTAN

Aral Sea

Lake Balkhash

TURKMENISTAN

UZBEKISTAN

SAMARKAND

KYRGYZSTAN

TAJIKISTAN

This colorful building is St. Basil's Cathedral in Moscow, the capital city of Russia.

Scale

0   500 miles

ARCTIC
OCEAN

S I B E R I A

Lena

Tunguska

Yenisei

Kamchatka
Peninsula

SEA OF
OKHOTSK

Sakhalin

Amur

Lake
Baikal

■ IRKUTSK

VLADIVOSTOK ■

Besides Russians,
about 100 different
peoples live in
Russia. This
Nenets woman
lives in the
Arctic region
of Siberia.

The
Siberian
crane is 60
inches tall. The
male bird
sometimes
performs a kind
of dance.

This is the great
gateway of an
ancient Islamic
building in
Samarkand, a city
in Uzbekistan.

Scale

0   300 miles

A whirling dervish from Turkey. A Muslim worshipper, he performs a special dance.

BLACK SEA

ISTANBUL

ANKARA

T U R K E Y

CASPIAN SEA

TABRIZ

KURDISTAN

CYPRUS

S Y R I A

TEHRAN

LEBANON

BEIRUT

I R A Q

Tigris

MEDITERRANEAN SEA

DAMASCUS

BAGHDAD

I R A N

Euphrates

JORDAN

SHIRAZ

JERUSALEM

ISRAEL

DID YOU KNOW ..?

The Kurds do not have a country of their own. Their land, Kurdistan, stretches across Turkey, Iraq and Iran.

KUWAIT

PERSIAN GULF

BAHRAIN

DUBAI

The Wailing Wall in Jerusalem is all that remains of an ancient Jewish temple. Many Jews go there to pray.

RIYADH

QATAR

UNITED ARAB EMIRATES

R E D   S E A

S A U D I   A R A B I A

JIDDAH

MECCA

Rub 'al Khali (Empty Quarter)

O M A N

SAN'A

Y E M E N

ARABIAN SEA

ADEN

THE MIDDLE EAST

SOUTHWESTERN ASIA is also known as the Middle East. Much of this region is very dry, although parts of the Mediterranean coast and the area lying between the Tigris and Euphrates rivers in Iraq are richly fertile. The world's earliest farming settlements grew up here. Turkey, Iran and Afghanistan are mountainous lands. Most of the Arabian Peninsula is desert.

MASHHAD

KABUL

AFGHANISTAN

MUSCAT

The Bedouin are nomads. They are a people who do not live in one place but wander with their animals across the desert lands of the Middle East.

The ancient city of San'a is the capital of Yemen. Lining its narrow, winding streets are these tall, carefully decorated houses. Built of stone and mud-brick with patterns made out of plaster, these early "skyscrapers" are hundreds of years old.

The countries near the Persian Gulf have vast deposits of oil. It is transported to other countries around the world in tankers like this one.

Puppet shows are popular in Java, Indonesia. The puppets are made out of flat cardboard and moved by wires.

Rice is the main crop of Southeast Asia. It is grown in waterlogged fields called paddies. In hilly areas, steps are built into the slopes so that the floodwaters do not flow away.

KASHMIR

LAHORE
PAKISTAN
Indus

DELHI

KARACHI
Thar Desert

VARANASI

H i m a l a y a s
NEPAL

BHUTAN

Ganges

BANGLADESH

KOLKATA (CALCUTTA)

DHAKA

MYANMAR (BURMA)

I N D I A

MUMBAI (BOMBAY)

Irrawaddy

BAY OF BENGAL

YANGON

CHENNAI (MADRAS)

Andaman Islands **(INDIA)**

SRI LANKA

COLOMBO

MALDIVES

"Giraffe-necked" women of Padaung, Burma, wear brass rings to make their necks grow longer.

For followers of the Hindu religion, the Ganges, like many of India's rivers, is a holy river. People have their ashes scattered in it after they die. Worshippers come to holy places, such as Varanasi, and bathe in the water.

INDIA AND SOUTHEAST ASIA

INDIA has the world's second largest population after China. Most of its people live in the countryside. India's best farmland is found in the plains of the River Ganges. To the north lie the Himalayas, the world's highest mountains. Across the Thar Desert in the east is Pakistan, another country with a large population.

Travelling east, we reach the tropical rainforests of Southeast Asia. In many parts, the trees are being felled to make way for farmland, cities, reservoirs or quarries.

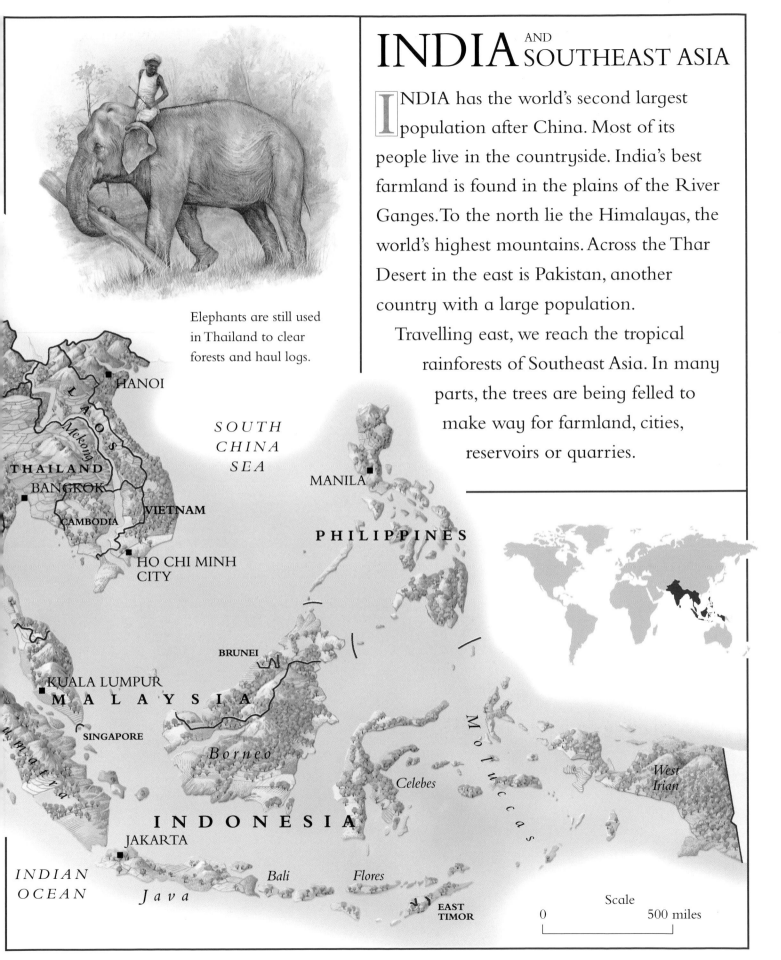

Elephants are still used in Thailand to clear forests and haul logs.

HANOI

LAOS

Mekong

THAILAND

BANGKOK

CAMBODIA

VIETNAM

HO CHI MINH CITY

SOUTH CHINA SEA

MANILA

PHILIPPINES

BRUNEI

KUALA LUMPUR

MALAYSIA

SINGAPORE

Sumatra

Borneo

Celebes

Moluccas

West Irian

INDONESIA

JAKARTA

INDIAN OCEAN

Java

Bali

Flores

EAST TIMOR

Scale

0   500 miles

CHINA AND JAPAN

CHINA has the largest population of any country in the world. About a fifth of the world's people live here. The mountains and deserts of the west are mostly empty. Eastern China has rich farmland and great cities. Japan is made up of four main islands. Thousands of earthquakes happen here every year.

DID YOU KNOW . . ?

The main language of China is Mandarin. There are many spoken versions, but only one kind of writing, which everyone can understand.

On some Chinese rivers, fishermen train cormorants to catch fish for them.

M O

G O

C H

Takla Makan

T I B E T

Himalayas

Salween

The Great Wall of China was built to stop raiders from the north invading China. The Wall is more than 1,800 miles long and is the largest structure ever built by people. It took many centuries to complete it.

In the Tibetan mountains, people live by herding yaks. This woman is churning yak's milk into butter.

Japan's capital, Tokyo, is one of the largest cities in the world. The subway trains are very crowded.

MANCHURIA

ULAN BATOR

OLIA

HARBIN

i

SEA OF JAPAN

SHENYANG

NORTH KOREA

BEIJING

PYONGYANG

JAPAN

TOKYO

INA

TIANJIN

KYOTO

SEOUL

OSAKA

SOUTH KOREA

LANZHOU

Huang

Grand Canal

YELLOW SEA

KITAKYUSHU

XI'AN

NANJING

SHANGHAI

WUHAN

Yangtse

HANGZHOU

EAST CHINA SEA

CHONGQING

Ryukyu Is (JAPAN)

UIYANG

TAIPEI

TAIWAN

GUANGZHOU

HONG KONG

Buddhism is one of the religions of Japan. A pagoda is a sacred place of Buddhist worship.

Scale

0   500 miles

Hainan

29

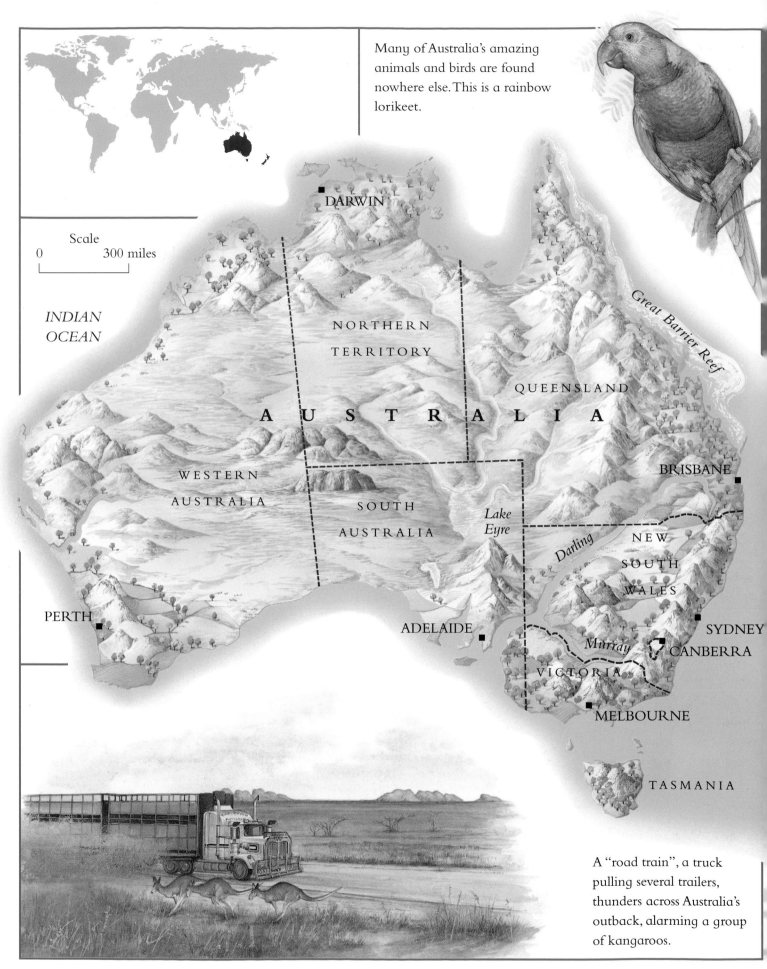

Many of Australia's amazing animals and birds are found nowhere else. This is a rainbow lorikeet.

Scale
0   300 miles

INDIAN OCEAN

DARWIN

NORTHERN
TERRITORY

QUEENSLAND

Great Barrier Reef

A U S T R A L I A

WESTERN
AUSTRALIA

SOUTH
AUSTRALIA

Lake Eyre

Darling

BRISBANE

NEW
SOUTH
WALES

PERTH

ADELAIDE

Murray

SYDNEY
CANBERRA

VICTORIA

MELBOURNE

TASMANIA

A "road train", a truck pulling several trailers, thunders across Australia's outback, alarming a group of kangaroos.

Sydney, Australia's largest city, is built around a natural harbor. Its most famous landmarks are the Harbour Bridge and the "sail-roofed" Opera House.

Sheep farming is very important in both Australia and New Zealand. Together, they have more than 200 million sheep! Here, a shearer removes the fleece of a Merino sheep.

AUSTRALIA AND NEW ZEALAND

AUSTRALIA and New Zealand are part of Oceania. This region also includes Papua New Guinea and the islands of the Pacific Ocean *(see pages 2-3)*.

Australia is large enough to be a continent itself. Nearly all its inhabitants live near the southeastern and south-western coasts. Here also are Australia's farmlands and vineyards. The rest of the country is almost empty. Most of the western and central regions, known as the outback, are dry grassland or desert.

New Zealand is made up of two large mountainous islands. Its warm, rainy climate is perfect for farming.

DID YOU KNOW . . ?

The Great Barrier Reef, just off Australia's northeast coast, is the world's largest living thing. More than 1,200 miles long, the reef is made of coral, the skeletons of tiny creatures. It is home to many kinds of fish.

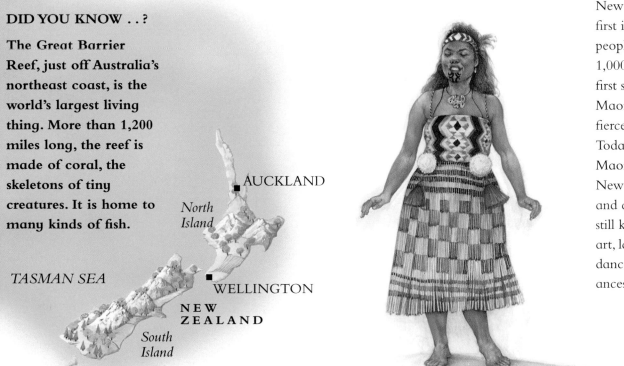

AUCKLAND

North Island

TASMAN SEA

WELLINGTON

N E W Z E A L A N D

South Island

New Zealand was first inhabited by people only about 1,000 years ago. The first settlers were the Maoris. They were fierce warriors. Today, people of Maori descent live in New Zealand's towns and cities. But they still keep alive the art, language and dances of their ancestors.

INDEX OF PLACE NAMES

Published in the United States, Canada, and Puerto Rico by Hammond World Atlas Corporation
Union, New Jersey 07083
www.hammondmap.com

Copyright © 2004 Orpheus Books Ltd

Created and produced by Orpheus Books Ltd

Illustrators Gary Hincks, Nicki Palin

ISBN 0-8437-1975-3

Printed and bound in Singapore.

ABBREVIATIONS USED IN THIS ATLAS

Br.	(Great) Britain
Fr.	France
I.	Island
Is.	Islands
L.	Lake
Mts.	Mountains
Pr.	Prince
US	United States